SCIENCE DISCOVERY

MAGNETS AND ELECTRICITY

Alan Ward

Franklin Watts

London • New York • Sydney • Toronto

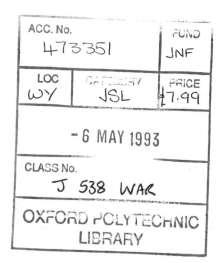
© 1992 Franklin Watts

Franklin Watts
96 Leonard Street
London EC2A 4RH

Franklin Watts Inc.
95 Madison Avenue
New York, NY 10016

Franklin Watts Australia
14 Mars Road
Lane Cove
New South Wales 2066

ISBN: 0 7496 0 679 7

Printed in Great Britain

A CIP catalogue record for this book
is available from the British Library

Series Editor : A. Patricia Sechi
Designer : Mike Snell
Illustrations : Alex Pang
Typesetting : Spectrum, London

CONTENTS

WHAT IS A MAGNET?

Some materials can pull metal objects towards them. These materials are called magnets. Magnets pull certain metals. A magnet can pull a steel paperclip.

What happens when you hold the magnet close to one of the paperclips? See if you can make your magnet pull a train of paperclips.

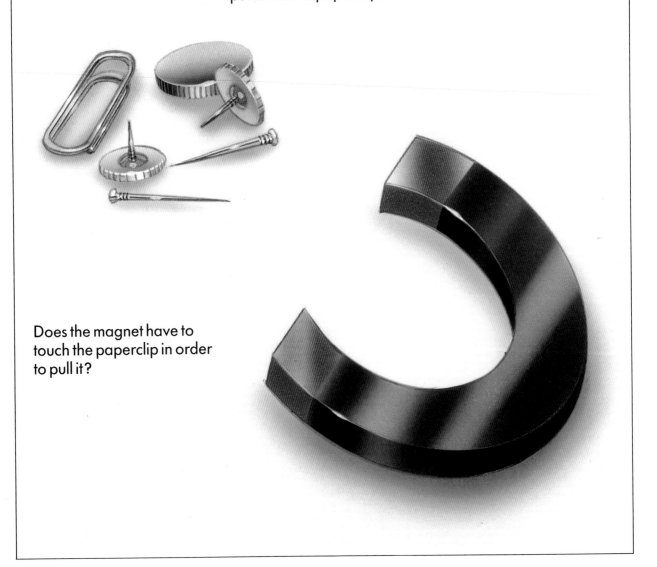

Does the magnet have to touch the paperclip in order to pull it?

The Indian rope trick

In this trick, a rope seemed to be able to hold itself upright in the air. You can try out your own versions of this trick.

YOU NEED:

- a metal paperclip
- cotton thread
- modelling clay
- a magnet

Cut a length of thread and push one end into a lump of modelling clay. Stick the clay to a table. Tie the paperclip to the other end of the thread. Now use the magnet to make the thread stand upright, but do not touch the paperclip!

Magnets can be made in different shapes and sizes. They can be bars, horseshoes or even disks.

Did you know?

There are magnets in use all around your home. The door of your refrigerator has a magnet which helps the door to close. Can you find this magnet by holding a steel paperclip close to the refrigerator door?

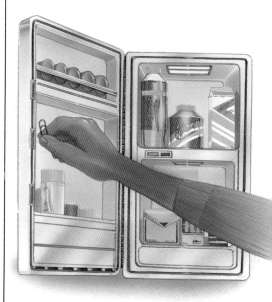

Use a paperclip to find magnets that may be hidden around your home, for instance inside cupboard doors.

Warning!

Keep magnets away from watches, televisions, video recorders and sound or video cassettes. Magnets will damage watches, televisions and video recorders. They also damage the special magnetic coating on video and sound cassettes so that the picture or sound is spoiled.

MAGNETIC MATERIALS

A magnet will only pull certain materials towards itself. The materials that a magnet will pull are called magnetic materials. Those materials which are not pulled by a magnet are called non-magnetic materials.

Find out which materials around you are magnetic and which are non-magnetic. Do some treasure hunting around your home.

Fill the box with sand and then hide the different objects in the sand.

Hold a magnet in your hand, then move your hand through the sand in the box. See which objects you can attract with the magnet. These objects are made from magnetic material. The objects which are left in the sand at the end of your hunt are made from non-magnetic material.

Most of the magnetic objects will be made out of metal. Can you find any metal objects which are not magnetic?

Did you know?
You can use a magnet to help you save the Earth's resources. Aluminium drinks cans can be recycled. You can find out which ones are aluminium because a magnet will not attract them. You can then take the cans to a collecting centre ready to be recycled.

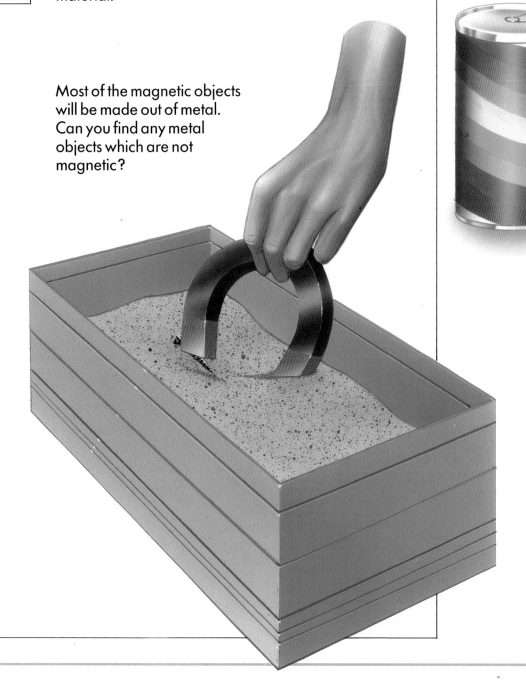

THE FORCE OF MAGNETISM

The force which makes magnetic materials attract other materials is called magnetism. Magnetism can act through different materials.

Place the paperclip on a table and cover it with a playing card. Can you still pick up the paperclip with the magnet? Now place a second playing card on top of the first one. Will the magnet still pick up the paperclip?

See how many playing cards you can get the force of magnetism to work through.

What other materials does the force of magnetism act through? Try doing your own tests on other materials, such as wool, aluminium foil, plastic, paper, nylon and other materials around you at home.

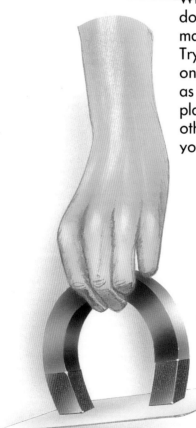

Magnetic boats

Ask an adult to cut a slice off the cork. (This is best done by sawing the cork with a sharp wet penknife.) Glue the paperclip to the bottom of the slice of cork. Cut out a paper sail and fix it to the top of the cork using a cocktail stick as the mast. You have now made your magnetic boat.

Place the dish or tray on the two piles of books, leaving space in between the two piles for your hand. Put some water in the dish or tray and place your boat in the water. Place the eggcups upside down in the water — these are the rocks in your lake.

YOU NEED:

- a steel paperclip
- a cork
- paper
- scissors
- glue
- a cocktail stick
- a shallow dish or tray (made of a non-magnetic material)
- water
- three or four eggcups
- two piles of books
- a magnet

Hold the magnet under the dish or tray and you will be able to steer your boat through the water and around the rocks.

MAGNETIC FORCE FIELDS

The space around a magnet where the force of magnetism acts is called a force field. Can you think of another kind of force which acts through space? A hint could be to think that 'what goes up must come down'!

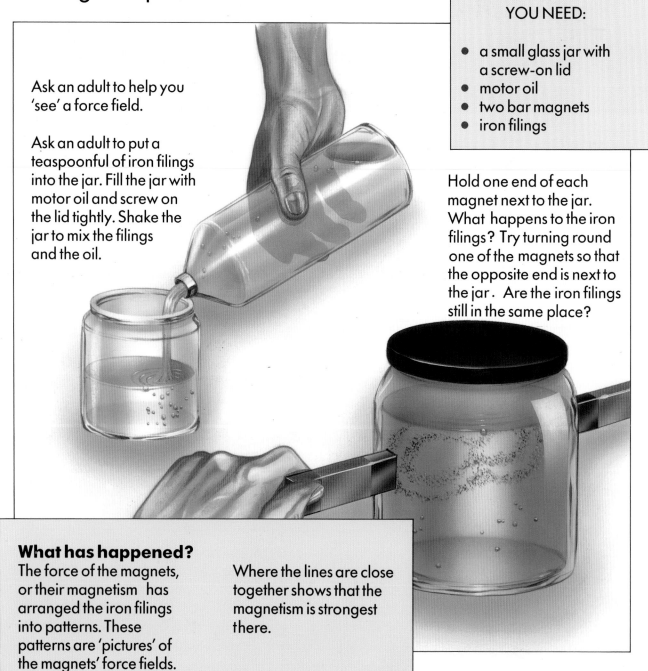

Ask an adult to help you 'see' a force field.

Ask an adult to put a teaspoonful of iron filings into the jar. Fill the jar with motor oil and screw on the lid tightly. Shake the jar to mix the filings and the oil.

Hold one end of each magnet next to the jar. What happens to the iron filings? Try turning round one of the magnets so that the opposite end is next to the jar. Are the iron filings still in the same place?

What has happened?
The force of the magnets, or their magnetism has arranged the iron filings into patterns. These patterns are 'pictures' of the magnets' force fields.

Where the lines are close together shows that the magnetism is strongest there.

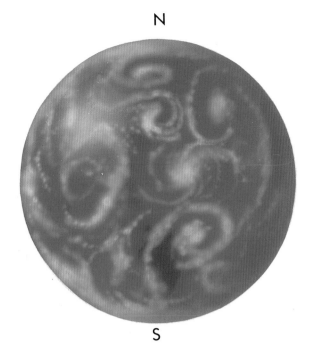

N

S

The Earth is a magnet

The Earth acts like a huge magnet. If an ordinary magnet is free to move, the Earth's magnetism pulls one of its ends and makes that end point towards the North Pole. The end of the magnet that does this is called the north-seeking pole, or the north pole for short. The other end of the magnet is called the south-seeking pole, or south pole for short. It is pulled towards the South Pole of the Earth.

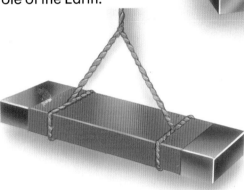

You can find out in which direction the North Pole lies. Tie a piece of string around the centre of a bar magnet and let it hang freely in the middle of a room. Be careful not to hang the magnet near magnetic materials or another magnet.

When the magnet stops moving, one of its ends will be pointing towards the North Pole. But how can you tell which one it is? If you do this in the middle of a sunny day, the Sun is in the south at midday.

Did you know?

Pigeons, bees, salmon and some other animals have tiny magnets inside their bodies. Scientists think that these animals have a kind of sense of the Earth's magnetism. This sense helps them to find their way.

MAGNETIC PULLS AND PUSHES

A magnet can pull another magnet towards itself, or it can push the other magnet away. When a magnet pulls another magnet, we say that it attracts the other magnet. When it pushes the other magnet away, we say that it repels the other magnet.

YOU NEED:

- two bar magnets
- paper
- scissors
- glue

The pull of a magnet is strongest at its two ends. These are the magnet's poles. Every magnet has a north-seeking, or north pole and a south-seeking, or south pole. Do you know which poles will attract each other, and which ones will push each other away?

Cut out two small circles of paper and stick them on the magnets to mark the north pole. Hold the two north poles a short distance from each other. What happens? Does a north-seeking pole pull or push away another north-seeking pole?

Do the magnets actually have to touch each other in order to pull or push away?

Using the two bar magnets, try and answer these questions.

Does a south-seeking pole pull or push away a north-seeking pole? Does a north-seeking pole pull or push away a south-seeking pole? Does a south-seeking pole pull or push away a south-seeking pole?

What has happened?
You have just worked out the rules, or laws, of magnetism. Two similar, or like, poles will push each other away. So a north-seeking pole will push away another north-seeking pole, and a south-seeking pole will push away another south-seeking pole.

Two opposite, or unlike, poles will pull toward each other. A north-seeking pole and a south-seeking pole will do this. A simple way of remembering these rules is to say:

Unlike poles attract each other.
Like poles repel each other.

Do you know how the Indian rope trick mentioned earlier was really done? In fact, a magnet was holding up the rope, which had another magnet hidden in its tip. The two like poles of the magnets attracted each other.

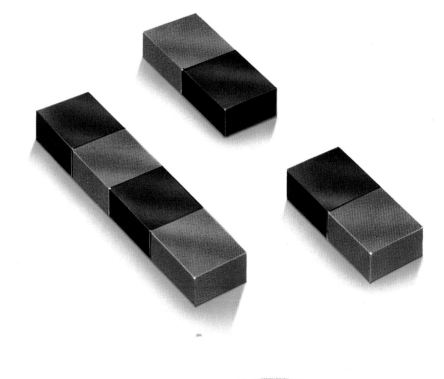

Did you know?

Trains with very powerful magnets underneath them can be made to float, or levitate above a track. The track contains another set of magnets. The magnets in the train repel the magnets in the track, and this force pushes the train along at very high speeds. These trains are called 'maglev' trains. What do you think 'maglev' stands for?

MAGNETS IN COMPASSES

Magnets are used in compasses. For hundreds of years magnetic compasses have helped sailors to find their way across oceans. A compass helps us to know in which direction we are travelling because it always shows where north and south lie.

You can make your own simple magnetic compass.

Stroke the magnet along the needle to make the needle magnetic. Stroke the magnet about 5 times, each time in the same direction.

Ask an adult to cut a slice off the cork. Float the cork in a bowl of water and place the magnetized needle on top of the cork. The needle will act like a compass and will point in a north-south direction.

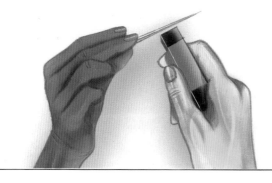

Did you know?
The Earth's magnetism can even magnetize household objects which are made from iron or steel. Use a compass to test metal food cans and other metal objects at home. Do they have a magnetic north-seeking pole and a magnetic south-seeking pole?

A magnetic trick

You need to make a magnetic pointer on a stand for this magnetic trick. Before doing the trick, you will have to find out in which direction north lies.

Stick a small ball of modelling clay to a tabletop. Push one needle in the clay and place the pen top over the tip of it. Stick a tiny ball of modelling clay on top of the pen top.

Magnetize the second needle as you did earlier, and position it across the top of the pen top. This is your magnetic pointer.

You need to find out which end of your needle is the north-seeking pole. Make sure you remember which end points to north. Now for the magic trick!

If you do not have picture cards, make your own. Mark the back of one card with two small black dots. Then place this card at the bottom of the pile. The cards should all be facing down.

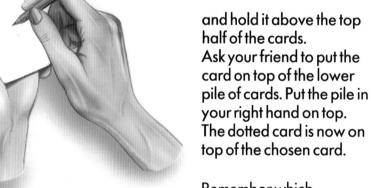

Ask a friend to pick a card and remember the picture. The friend should show it to everyone, except you. Now, in your right hand take the bottom half of the pile of cards, with the dotted one at the bottom

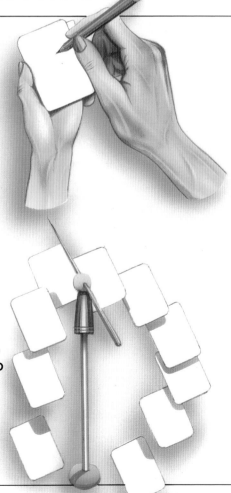

and hold it above the top half of the cards. Ask your friend to put the card on top of the lower pile of cards. Put the pile in your right hand on top. The dotted card is now on top of the chosen card.

Remember which direction is north. Place all the cards, face down, in a circle. Make sure that you place the card after the dotted one in the part of the circle which faces north. Put your pointer in the middle of the circle and spin it round.

When it stops spinning, turn the cards over – the chosen one last. It's magic!

15

ELECTRICITY

Warning

Electricity can be very dangerous. Never connect a wire to the mains electricity sockets in your house. Always use a low-volt battery for your electricity experiments.

Electric current is energy on the move. It can work things such as lights, toys, some magnets, motors and doorbells. Any material that lets an electric current pass through it is called a conductor.

Any material that does not allow an electric current to pass through it is called an insulator. Insulators are sometimes called non-conductors.

Insulating materials are used to cover conducting materials. They stop the electricity from escaping and doing harm. The plastic coating around electric wires is an insulating material.

How does electricity move?

Most of the electricity that we use has to move around in circuits. An electric circuit is like a circle, with no beginning and no end. Imagine a circle of string which can be bent into any shape. Electricity does not have to move in a circle — it can flow in any shape.

Bend the piece of card in half. Cut a small circle out of the middle of the top half of the card. Screw the light bulb into the hole. Tape a piece of foil on the inside of the card so that the bottom of the bulb will touch it when the card is closed.

YOU NEED:

- a piece of thick card, about 15 centimetres long and 10 centimetres wide
- scissors
- a 1.25 or 1.5 volt torch bulb
- two pieces of plastic-coated wire, about 30 centimetres long
- a 1.5 volt battery
- aluminium foil
- sticky tape
- a rubber band

Ask an adult to help you cut off about 2 centimetres of plastic coating at each end of the two wires. Tape the end of one wire to the metal part of the bulb. Tape the other end to the bottom of the battery. Tape one end of the second wire to the top of the battery, and tape the other end to the aluminium foil.

Put a tight-fitting rubber band around the ends of the battery to make good connections. When you close the card, the light will come on.

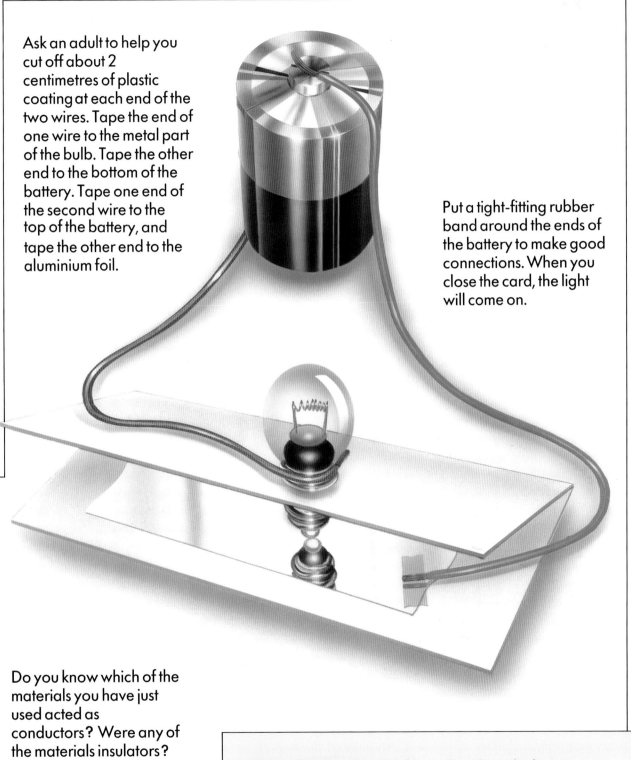

Do you know which of the materials you have just used acted as conductors? Were any of the materials insulators?

What has happened?
When you close the card, the bottom of the bulb touches the aluminium foil. This makes the electric circuit complete. The electric current can now flow from the battery, along the wire to the foil, through the foil to the bulb and then along the second wire and back to the battery. You have just made an electric circuit.

ELECTRICITY AND MAGNETISM

Electricity and magnetism act on each other. When an electric current flows along a wire, it makes a weak magnetic force field. This force field is called electromagnetism.

Magnet power

Ask an adult to help you cut about 2 centimetres of the plastic coating from each end of the wire. Tape one bare end of wire to one of the metal ends, or terminals, of the battery.

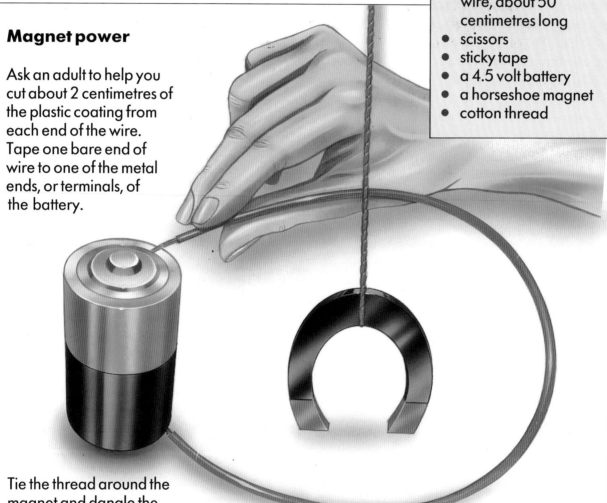

Tie the thread around the magnet and dangle the magnet near the wire. What happens? Now, just for a second hold the other end of the wire against the second terminal of the battery. What happens to the magnet this time?

What has happened?

When both ends of the wire are connected to the battery, electricity flows along the wire. This electricity, or electric current, makes the magnet move. The magnetic force field around the electric wire is acting on the magnet's own force field. It can push or pull the magnet.

Jumping foil snake

You can make a strip of aluminium kitchen foil turn into a jumping snake.

Ask an adult to help you cut off about 2 centimetres of plastic coating from both ends of each piece of wire. Tape the end of one wire to one of the battery terminals.

Tape one end of the other wire to the second battery terminal.

Cut out a strip of aluminium foil about one centimetre wide and 40 centimetres long. Place the aluminium strip on the table.

Stand the horseshoe magnet over the middle of the strip, like an arch. Now touch the free ends of the wires to each end of the foil strip. Do this only for a second. What happens to the foil?

What has happened?

When the ends of the wires are connected to the aluminium snake, an electric current flows through it. This creates a magnetic field around the foil. The magnetism of the foil acts on the magnetism of the magnet.

When the snake jumps up under the magnet, it is attracted to the magnet. When it pushes away from the magnet, it is repelled by it.

MAGNETS AND MOTORS

Electricity and magnetism are mysterious forces. Scientists know when electricity and magnetism are acting and they know what these two forces can do, but we don't know exactly what they are.

A magnet can make the needle of a compass spin round. Put a compass on the table. Hide a strong magnet in your hand. Wave your hand above the compass, but do not touch it. You can make the needle of the compass spin round. Is your magnet strong enough to make the compass needle spin if you hold the magnet under the table?

What has happened?
The pushes and pulls of magnetism are acting through space. Magnets do not have to touch each other for their forces to act on each other. Magnetism can also pass through the flesh and bones of your hand, as well as through the wood of a table.

Magnets inside electric motors can make part of the motor spin round.

Stick a lump of modelling clay on the table and push the needle into it. Balance the cake cup upside-down on the needle. Gently place the upturned jug or bowl over the cake cup. Tie the thread around the magnet and spin the magnet above the upturned jug or bowl. Does the cake cup move?

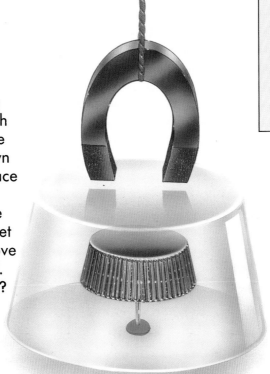

What has happened?

The force field of the spinning magnet causes a weak electric current in the aluminium cake cup. The magnetic force and electric current produce electromagnetism. This electromagnetism makes the cake cup spin round. In fact the cup becomes a magnet itself, pulled around by the magnet spinning above it.

Did you know?

The idea of the spinning cake cup is used to make the small motors which are found inside car speedometers and electricity meters.

Can you think of anything in your house which has an electric motor to make it work?

ELECTROMAGNETS

Electromagnets are only magnetic when an electric current flows through them. When the electricity is switched off, they are no longer magnetic. Electromagnets are used to pick up metals and metal objects. You can make your own electromagnetic crane.

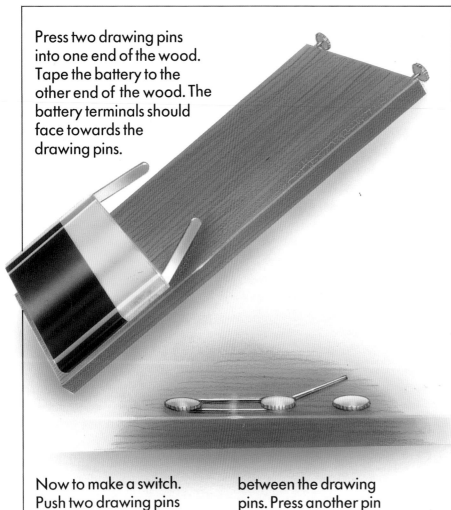

Press two drawing pins into one end of the wood. Tape the battery to the other end of the wood. The battery terminals should face towards the drawing pins.

Ask an adult to help you cut about 7 centimetres off the piece of wire. You now have two wires. Ask the adult to help you cut about 2 centimetres of plastic coating off the ends of both wires.

Wind the long wire around the steel nail to make a coil. Leave about 50 centimetres of wire hanging free at each end. Use sticky tape to keep the coiled wire in place.

Tape one end of the long wire to the battery terminal which is furthest away from the switch. Tape the other end of the wire to one of the drawing pins on the switch.

Now to make a switch. Push two drawing pins into the wood near the battery. Open out one end of the paperclip. Fix it between the drawing pins. Press another pin into the wood near the opened end of the paperclip.

Did you know?

Inside electric motors is a coil of wire on a rod. A magnet surrounds the coil of wire. When an electric current flows in the coil, the magnetic force in the coil pushes and pulls the surrounding magnet. These pushes and pulls make the motor spin. In some motors the magnet spins; in other motors the coil spins.

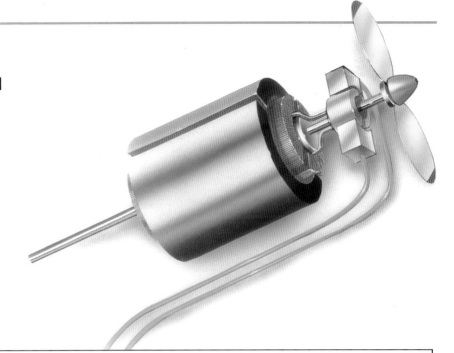

Tape one end of the short wire to the free battery terminal and join the other end to the paperclip on the switch. Loop the long wire around the pins on the end of the piece of wood.

Press the end of the paperclip so it touches the drawing pin beside it. This makes the electric current flow round.

The electricity flows through the coil of wire and makes the nail into a magnet.

When you lift the end of the paperclip away from the drawing pin, this switches off the electricity and the nail loses its magnetism. Now see what you can pick up with your electromagnetic crane.

Do not turn on your switch for more than 2 or 3 seconds at a time.

WHAT IS STATIC ELECTRICITY?

Electric current flows along wires and through conductors. But electricity can also stay in one place. This kind of electricity is called static electricity. It is made when things rub together.

Rub the balloon with the woollen cloth. It is best to do this when the air around you is dry. A cold and frosty day would be a good time. You could use a woollen scarf to rub the balloon.

Now hold your balloon up against a wall or ceiling. What happens?

While you are rubbing the balloon, you should hear tiny crackling sounds. These are really tiny sparks of electricity. When you rub the balloon with the cloth, the balloon becomes charged, with static electricity. This makes the balloon pull itself up towards the ceiling. How long does it stay there?

Did you know?

Inside a thunder cloud are crystals of ice, tiny drops of water, smoky dirt and dust. All these particles, or tiny pieces are rubbed together by fierce winds. When this happens, the cloud becomes charged with static electricity.

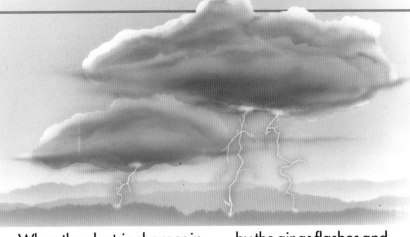

When the electric charges in the cloud are powerful enough, they are conducted by the air as flashes and sparks of lightning.

Electric straws

If your fingers are clean and dry, you can use them to charge a plastic straw with static electricity.

YOU NEED:

- plastic straws
- a plastic tray

Stroke a straw several times with your finger. Can you make it cling upright to a window? Hold a competition with your friends to find out which of you can make a straw cling to the window for the longest time.

Charge a straw by rubbing it and place it across a plastic tray. You can use a tray that contained food from a supermarket. Make sure you clean it first. Now charge another straw and hold it next to the straw on the tray. Amazingly, the other straw rolls away. Use the straw in your hand to keep pushing the other straw backwards and forwards. The straws, tray and window must all be dry, otherwise the activity will not work.

POSITIVE AND NEGATIVE CHARGES

All materials are made up of two kinds of electric substance called charges. There are two kinds of charges — positive and negative. They behave in a similar way to the poles of a magnet. Opposite charges, such as negative and positive charges, attract each other. Similar charges such as negative and negative charges repel each other.

When a material has too many of one kind of charge we say it has static electricity.

When materials are rubbed together negative charges are often rubbed off one material and onto the other material. When you rubbed the balloon with the woollen cloth, extra negative charges were rubbed onto the balloon. These extra negative charges pushed away the negative charges

Find out what you can attract by charging a plastic comb with static electricity.
Rub the comb with the woollen cloth. In dry weather, the comb will do some magical things!

YOU NEED:

- a plastic comb
- a piece of woollen cloth
- a ping-pong ball
- salt
- pepper
- a cotton thread, 10 centimetres long
- water

See if the comb will pull along a ping-pong ball.

Will it pull the pepper grains out from a mixture of salt and pepper?

Can you make a piece of cotton thread wriggle like a snake?

Make your own hair stand on end.

Can you bend a trickle of water with your comb?

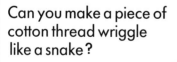

What do you think made the plastic straw move about on the tray?

on the ceiling. Then the balloon's negative charges pulled towards the positive charges left and the balloon was attracted to the ceiling.

YOU NEED:

- tissue paper
- scissors
- an aluminium foil dish
- a piece of clear plastic
- two books
- a woollen cloth

Electric dancers

Cut out some shapes of people from the tissue paper. The figures should be about 3 centimetres tall.

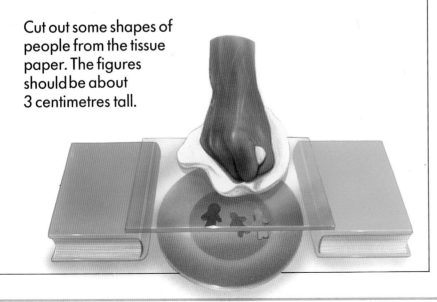

Put the paper people in the dish and place a book on each side of the dish. Make a low bridge over the dish by resting the plastic on the books.

Now rub the plastic with the woollen cloth. This will make the paper people dance about.

Did you know?
When you take off a woollen sweater, you may rub negative charges from the wool onto your hair. This charges your hair with extra negative charges, but your sweater now has too many positive charges. The opposite charges pull towards each other so the sweater attracts your hair making it stand on end. What a hair-raising experience!

EXTRA PROJECTS

Magnetic force

You can put on your own theatre show using magnets to make paper characters move around on a stage.

The stage can be made from a cardboard box which you can decorate. Cut a large hole out of one of the long sides of the box. This is the front of the theatre.

Cut out the bottom of the box and raise it about 3-4 centimetres. Stick it to the sides of the box.

Draw characters on the card. Leave a plain strip of card, about 3 centimetres deep at the bottom of each character. Cut out the characters and fold the strip of card so that they stand up. Glue a paperclip to the folded part to make the characters magnetic.

YOU NEED:

- a shoebox or similar shaped box
- a piece of cardboard
- a piece of stiff card
- scissors
- glue
- coloured pens
- steel paperclips
- a bar magnet
- a small stick

Use sticky tape to attach the magnet to the end of the stick. Slide this below the stage. You will be able to move the characters around with this stick. Now, on with the show!

Static electricity

You can use static electricity to help ring your own home-made bell.

Stand each tin on an upturned plastic tray. Tie one end of the thread to the paperclip. Tie the other end around the remaining plastic tray. Place the tray across the top of the tins so that the paperclip dangles between the tins.

Rub the balloon with the woollen cloth. Now hold the balloon next to one of the tins. The paperclip will swing backwards and forwards, making the tins ring like a bell.

YOU NEED:

- three plastic food trays
- two empty food tins
- a steel paperclip
- cotton thread
- a balloon
- a woollen cloth

Electric circuits

Tape one end of the bare wire to a flat surface. Tape the other end to one of the battery terminals. Bend the wire into several curves.

Ask an adult to help you cut about 3 centimetres of plastic coating from each end of the insulated wires. Tape the end of one wire to the free battery terminal. Attach the other end to one of the terminals on the bulb holder.

Attach one end of the last piece of wire to the other terminal of the bulb holder. Bend the other end of the wire in a loop around the bare wire. Can you move the loop along the bent wire without making the bulb light up?

If the wire loop touches the bent wire the circuit is completed and so the bulb will light up. The loop acts as a kind of switch to close the circuit and switch on the electricity.

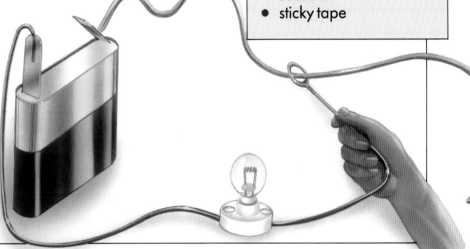

Electric motors

Attach the paperclips around the edge of the lid. Make a hole in the centre of the lid. Cut the clip off the pen top and push the top up through the hole in the lid. This makes a kind of bearing for the needle.

Stick a lump of modelling clay to a table and push the needle into the clay. Carefully balance the box lid on the needle.

Can you make the lid spin round by holding a bar magnet near the lid? What happens if you move the magnet backwards and forwards?

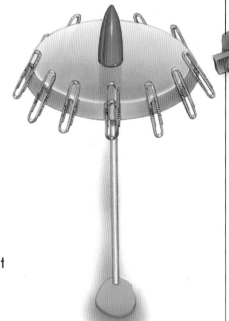

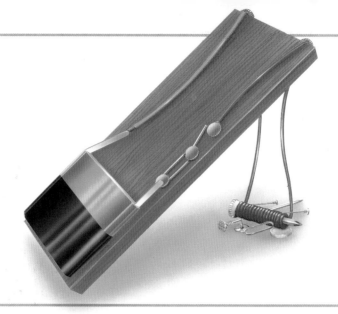

GLOSSARY

A

attract
To pull towards.

B

battery
A container filled with different chemicals which act on each other. The chemicals set free energy in the form of an electric current.

C

compass
A box that contains a magnetized needle. The needle is attracted by a magnetic force so that it points towards the North Pole and the South Pole. A compass is used to help people find their way across land and sea.

conductor
Any material that allows an electric current to flow through it easily.

E

electric charge
An invisible electric substance that is found in all materials. The two kinds of electric charge are positive charges and negative charges.

electric circuit
The continuous path which electric current flows along.

electric motor
A machine which changes electrical energy into motion. An electric motor is made to spin by magnetic forces.

electricity
A kind of energy that is made up of positive charges and negative charges. When electricity flows along wires it is called electric current.

electromagnetism
Magnetism which acts when an electric current flows.

F

filing
A tiny piece of iron.

force field
The space in which a force such as magnetism or electricity acts.

I

insulator
Any material that stops electric current escaping from a conductor.

L

levitate
To float.

M

magnet
An object made of metal or a brittle black substance which can push away another magnet and pull certain materials called magnetic substances.

magnetism
Invisible pulls and pushes that can act across space and through some materials.

N

North Pole
The part of the Earth that lies directly under the star called Polaris, or the Pole Star. The North Pole is the most northern point on the Earth's surface.

north-seeking pole
The end of a magnet which is pulled towards the Earth's North Pole.

R

repel
To push away.

S

South Pole
The most southern point on the Earth's surface.

south-seeking pole
The end of a magnet which is pulled towards the Earth's South Pole.

static electricity
Electricity that collects in one place. Static electricity exists when one kind of electric charge is not cancelled out by the opposite kind of electric charge.

T

terminal
The metal parts of a battery where wires are attached to the battery. Each battery has a positive terminal (marked +) and a negative terminal (marked −).

INDEX